IÑIGO

The Life of St. Ignatius Loyola for Young Readers

Written by J. Janda

Illustrated by Christopher L. Fay

PAULIST PRESS
New York/Mahwah, NJ

Library of Congress Cataloging-in Publication Data

Janda, J. (James), 1936-
    Iñigo: the life of St. Ignatius Loyola for young readers / by J. Janda: illustrated by Christopher L. Fay.
        p.   cm.
    ISBN 0-8091-6620-8 (pbk.)
    1. Ignatius, of Loyola, Saint, 1491-1556—Juvenile literature. 2. Jesuits—History—16th century—Juvenile literature. 3. Christian saints—Spain—Biography—Juvenile literature. [1. Ignatius, of Loyola, Saint, 1491-1556. 2. Saints.] I. Fay, Christopher L., ill. II. Title.
BX4700.L7J36   1994
271′.5302—dc20
[B]   94-34749
                                                               CIP
                                                                AC

Published by Paulist Press
997 Macarthur Boulevard
Mahwah, NJ 07430

Printed and bound in the
United States of America

Soli Dei Gloria

Acknowledgment

Grateful acknowledgment is hereby made for permission to quote "Thee God, I come from, to thee go," from *The Poems of Gerard Manley Hopkins,* Fourth Edition, edited by W.H. Gardner and N.H. MacKenzie. Copyright © The Society of Jesus and Oxford University Press, 1967.

Foreword

St. Ignatius of Loyola was born in the Basque country in northern Spain on December 24, 1491; he died July 31, 1556.

I have read many wonderful biographies of him and much of his work, but most of it was too difficult for young readers to understand—that is why I have written IÑIGO. This little book is simply an introduction. It is not the whole story of Saint Ignatius, but just enough for young readers to enjoy. When they are older, they may read more complete works about this man.

I would like to thank Christopher Fay, Karen Scialabba, and Marci Mayer whose encouragement, suggestions, and corrections helped me to present to you—IÑIGO.

Table of Contents

Book 1: The Early Years

Book 2 : Pamplona

Book 3 : A New Life

Book 1

The Early Years

Thee, God, I come from, to thee go,
All day long I like fountain flow
From thy hand out, swayed about
Mote-like in thy mighty glow.

What I know of thee I bless,
As acknowledging thy stress
On my being and as seeing
Something of thy holiness.

Gerard Manley Hopkins

1. María de Garín

"**M**AMA, MAMA, Don Beltrán is coming down the road. He is carrying something. Maybe it is for us," shouted the little girl as she ran into the cottage.

"He is? Are you sure?" asked María, her mother. María was carrying her baby who was too young to walk. She ran to the window and looked out. Sure enough, it was Don Beltrán de Loyola walking slowly down the road to her cottage.

"Here," said María to her little girl, "you hold your baby brother. I must clean off the table and put out some bread and cheese. It isn't every day that Don Beltrán de Loyola comes to visit us."

The little girl took the baby from her mother and sat on one of the benches. She held him on her lap while her mother hurriedly wiped off the table and put out plates of bread and cheese for Don Beltrán.

As María went to the cupboard to find the bottle of wine, the little girl's older brother opened the door and shouted, "Mama, mama, Don Beltrán is coming to see us and he is carrying a baby—and a big sack."

"A baby?" asked María. "Are you sure?"

3

"Yes," said the little boy. "I saw it with my own eyes. I ran up the road to meet him. He told me to tell you he is coming here. He looked as if he was crying."

"Don Beltrán was crying?" asked María, but before the boy could answer, she added, "Close the door. Don't let the cold air in."

The boy closed the door. As he turned, María handed him a towel. "Here," she said, "wipe off your face. Your nose is running. We must look our best for Don Beltrán. He has always been so kind to all of us—especially to your father. Don Beltrán is a generous man, always bringing us apples, cherries, chestnuts. Now, mind you, behave yourselves while he is here. No fighting. No complaining."

María de Garín was the young mother of these three children. Her husband was the local blacksmith. Their cottage was about a half-mile from the House of Loyola which had stood on the hill for generations.

Don Beltrán lived here and could trace his famous family back for hundreds of years. The Loyolas were well known everywhere. They were lords and ladies—nobility. They were known for their bravery. They could boast of many sons who had fought in battles in the services of the Kings and Queens of Spain.

And they were a generous family, too. Their coat of arms was a shield of gold, with red bands on one side, and a black kettle suspended between two wolves on the other side. It was said that the House of Loyola was so generous, they even fed the wolves.

2. Don Beltrán's Surprise Visit

There was a knock on the door. María smoothed out her apron, opened the door, and bowed. "Don Beltrán," she said, "please come in."

Don Beltrán slowly walked in and sat down on the bench next to the table opposite the little girl holding her baby brother.

After María closed the door, Don Beltrán put a sack on the floor; then he opened the blanket around the baby he was carrying. The baby had red hair.

"María," he began, "I have a favor to ask of you." His eyes welled up with tears. "This is my wife's tenth child. My wife," he swallowed hard, "has died."

"Your wife has died?" asked María, in disbelief.

"Yes," he said, "soon after he was baptized. He needs a mother to love and nurse him. That is why I have brought him to you. Can you do this for me? I shall reward you."

"Of course," said María, as she took the red haired baby from him. "What is her name?"

"His name," corrected Don Beltrán. "His name is Iñigo, Iñigo López de Loyola. In this sack are some apples and chestnuts for your family."

He got up to leave.

Then he turned to María and said, "Iñigo is my last child. Take good care of him. His brothers and sisters could never give him the care you could. And I want him to be closer to children his own age."

"I will care for him as my own child, I promise you—and teach him his prayers," said María, then sadly added, "No newborn must be without a mother."

Don Beltrán placed a gold coin on the table, then turned to leave.

"I am so very sorry to hear your wife has died," continued María. "I will pray for her and your family."

"She went back home. She is with God," he said. "We should be happy, no?" Then he went out, closing the door gently behind him, and slowly began the walk back up the road to the House of Loyola.

3. De Garín, the Blacksmith

The plates of bread and cheese were still on the table—along with a pitcher of milk—when María's husband came home from work. María was sitting in his big chair nursing the red-haired Iñigo.

Before he could kiss his children, they were all shouting, "Papa, papa, we have a new baby. His name is Iñigo."

"Oh?" said Garín. "Your mother didn't tell me." Then he smiled to María and said, "What have you there? Did God bless us with another child in only one day?"

"It is all very sad," she said. "Poor Don Beltrán. His wife is dead. She died soon after this child was baptized. He asked me to nurse him. I couldn't say no. Every baby needs a mother—and our children will help out."

"Marína de Licona is dead?" he asked. "When did that happen? I can't believe that."

"I really don't know. I think maybe yesterday."

"No," he said.

"Yes," said María.

"Papa, we will all help to take care of him,"

said his son. "We can watch him and play with him."

"Yes, papa," added his daughter, who was still holding her baby brother. "You always tell us to do what we can when someone needs help."

"Yes," said Garín. "This baby is in our hands now. I expect all of us to help your mother. Now, let us sit down and eat. I'm hungry. María, come, join us at the table. We have a great deal to talk about."

"Iñigo has just fallen asleep. You and the children eat. Everything is already on the table."

As Garín sat down, he noticed the gold coin on the table. "What's this?" he asked, picking it up. "It is gold."

"Don Beltrán left it for us," said María. "He is a very generous man."

4. Iñigo's Second Mother

Late that night, after the children and her husband were sound asleep, María got up to nurse Iñigo because he had started crying. She picked him up, carried him to Garín's big chair, sat down, and nursed him till he fell asleep.

"Hush, little baby. Don't cry. Your mama is in Heaven watching over you. I will be your second mother. I will love you and take care of you. Don't cry. God put you here for a reason. I don't know what that might be, but who am I to question God's will?"

"Do you know why you are here?" she asked, as she looked into his clear bright eyes. "I can see that you know; yes, you know. You know what God wants you to do. Can't you tell me? No? Well, I understand. My house is your house as long as God sees fit."

5. María Keeps Her Promise

And María was true to her promise to Don Beltrán—she took care of Iñigo as her own son. She nursed him, bathed him, dressed him, and, when her other children teased him and made him cry, she would say, "Be good to him. Don't tease him. He is our gift from God."

When he cried, she would hold him and talk to him till he fell asleep. "Don't cry, little one," she would say. "God's angels are watching over you. When you are afraid, say, 'Angel of God, my guardian dear, to whom His love commits me here. Ever this day be at my side to light and guard, to rule and guide. Amen.'"

Then came the day when Iñigo took his first steps. When Garín came home from work, his daughter shouted, "Papa, Iñigo can walk. He took his first steps alone today. Watch."

Then to Iñigo, she said, "Walk, Iñigo. Show papa how you can walk."

And Iñigo took his first steps alone. Garín caught him just before he lost his balance, lifted him high, and said, "Iñigo, today you took your first steps. Tomorrow you will be riding a horse. And the next day you will go to battle and hear those cannons go 'boom-boom, boom-boom, boom-boom!'"

And Iñigo laughed, and the children laughed, too.

"Enough," said María. "Everybody, sit down. It is time to eat. But first we pray."

Then Garín said, "Thank you, Lord, for this food, my wife and children, this house, and Iñigo. And bless old Don Beltrán for helping us out, Amen."

6. *Don Beltrán's Visits*

Yes, the next seven years were happy ones for María, her children, her husband, the blacksmith, and, of course, Iñigo.

Often you could see Don Beltrán coming down the road to visit the Garíns and talk to his son, Iñigo. As he watched him grow and play with María's children, he knew in his heart that he had made the right decision.

He would pick him up and hold him on his lap and talk to the little boy. He knew that somehow children understand things—even before they can find words to talk.

When Iñigo was three years old, Don Beltrán knew that Iñigo was beginning to understand the accomplishments of his older brothers.

"Iñigo, guess what," he said. "Christopher Columbus came back to Spain. He said he discovered a New World. And he is going back again. Your brave brother Juan is going with him. He is going as a soldier and will protect him if anything bad happens."

"Tell me again!" begged Iñigo. "Tell me again about my brave brother Juan."

"Your brother Juan," his father replied, "is a

strong soldier. He will protect Christopher Columbus on his dangerous and daring journeys."

Don Beltrán was always honest with Iñigo. When the time came to tell him the sad news of the death of his two brothers, Juan and Beltrán, Jr., he told the story simply: "They were fighting the French—for Spain. But they died a hero's death." Iñigo was only five when they died. He had never even met them.

Yet, there was happiness to share, also. Just before Iñigo was seven years old, Don Beltrán proudly told him that his brother Martín had just married Magdalena de Araoz.

"Iñigo," he said, "this Magdalena is a very good lady. Over the years, she was maid of honor to Queen Isabella and one of her favorites. She is going to move into our House of Loyola. You must meet her. The Queen gave her many gifts. You should see them.

"Magdalena and Martín want you to come and live there with them. They will be the new lord and lady of Loyola.

"I am getting too old to do much anymore. Martín will take over everything for me and oversee our lands. He told me he wants to meet you. I think you will be good friends. He wants you to move back home.

"It is time for you to learn to read and write. I have my plans for you. I want you to be a cleric, a priest. It will all be arranged. You will do it, no?

To the honor of the House of Loyola? You don't have to decide now, but think about it. I will not force you."

7. The Decision

As you might suspect, Don Beltrán's news was hard for the whole Garín family, but especially María. She had always loved him as her own son, but she also knew that Iñigo had to make the decision on his own. She told him, "Pray, Iñigo. Ask God what He wants you to do. He will put the answer in your heart. God has something special in mind for you. From the first day I laid eyes on you I felt this, but what that might be, I still don't know."

Weeks went by; then one day Iñigo said, "María, I think I should go back to the House of Loyola. I will miss you and Garín. You both have been a mother and father to me. And I will miss your children—my brothers and sisters. But I can always come back and play with them and see you, too."

"I understand," said María, as she hugged him. "If it doesn't work out, you know you will always have a home with us."

And so, on his seventh birthday, Iñigo moved back to the home of his father, old Don Beltrán, back to the House of Loyola.

8. The House of Loyola

That night, Martín and Magdalena and old Beltrán had a big surprise for Iñigo. It was his seventh birthday and they had secretly invited the whole Garín family to come to dinner—to celebrate Iñigo's birthday.

When Martín and Magdalena led Iñigo into the dining hall of Loyola, there were María, the children, and Garín—all wishing him a happy birthday. Old Beltrán was there, too, standing at the head of the big table glowing with candles and lots of food and a glass of wine at each place.

"Iñigo, my son, seat your guests. Martín, Magdalena, and I wanted to do something special for the Garín family—for all that they did for you—and welcome you to the House of Loyola."

Iñigo was very surprised—and very embarrassed, too. He whispered to his older brother, "Martín, what should I do?"

Martín smiled and whispered back, "Just tell the people to sit where they want to." And so Iñigo announced, "Everybody, sit where you want to."

And when everybody was seated, old Beltrán raised his glass of wine and said, "I propose a toast—to the Garín family—for all that they did

for my son Iñigo. And to Iñigo—on his seventh birthday."

Then everyone said, "Salud," clinked glasses, and drank to the health of Iñigo and the Garín family.

9. Magdalena and Martín

For the next nine years, Iñigo lived in the House of Loyola. He got to meet his sisters Juana, Petronilla, and Sancha. He got to know his other brothers Hernando, Ochoa, and Pero. Pero would eventually become a priest.

But he spent most of his time with Martín and Magdalena (it was not that he didn't like his other brothers and sisters, it's just that he felt closer to them).

Martín would often take him riding on a mule to see the farmland, orchards, and small shrines belonging to the House of Loyola. On these rides, Martín would introduce Iñigo to the farmers and their families whose ancestors had lived on the land for hundreds of years.

And Martín would tell him stories about his mother and father, his grandfather, his great-grandfather, even his great-great-great-grandfather.

"We have always been at war with the French, Iñigo," he said on one of the rides. "Always they are attacking our border towns and always we are defending them for Spain. We have been doing this forever."

Then to Iñigo's surprise, he got off his mule,

tied it to a tree, and with a loud voice, sang to the hills:

"Beotibar, Beotibar, Juan rode
With his sons to Beotibar.
The French saw their swords
And could not ignore
The proud Loyolas at Beotibar.

"Beotibar, Beotibar, seven sons
Were with Juan at Beotibar.
The French, they wished well
Then sent them to hell,
Juan Peréz and sons at Beotibar."

He bowed to Iñigo and laughed. Iñigo laughed, too.

"Is that song true?" asked Iñigo.

"Of course," said Martín, as he untied and mounted his mule.

"When did that all happen?" asked Iñigo.

"I don't know," said Martín—"a very long time ago. Follow me. The sun is going down. It is time to head home and eat."

It was times like this that Iñigo got close to his brother.

And he learned to read and write with the clerics at the school in town, but he didn't care much for studying—or to become a priest. Becoming a knight at court is what interested him. He loved to hear stories of travel, of bravery, of how his brothers, Juan and Beltrán, Jr., had died a hero's death in battle.

Yes, little by little, Iñigo began to feel at home at the House of Loyola. Magdalena was like a mother to him. She was so kind to him. She treated him as her own son, as María had done. She would tell him stories of her life at court, all about Queen Isabella—who died when Iñigo was thirteen—and King Ferdinand and the proud history of Spain. This is what he would love to hear.

She would also tell him stories from the Bible, and read to him from her book of Saints. This did not interest him much, but he would listen patiently.

She would often tell him, "Iñigo, always remember that God made each of us to know Him, to love Him, and to serve Him. Nothing else counts but God.

"I believe God has great plans for you. But you must never forget to say your prayers. If you pray, you can never lie to yourself—or sell your soul to anyone. Stay close to God. Always pray to him." Iñigo did not understand what "sell your soul to anyone" meant, but he was afraid to ask.

10. *Don Beltrán's Proposal*

Then, when Iñigo was fifteen, Don Beltrán took Iñigo aside and said, "Iñigo, I have done all I could for you. I feel God will soon call me back home, so I must tell you some things.

"You will soon become a man. I thought you would like to be a priest, but I can see that this does not interest you. Am I correct?"

"Yes," said Iñigo.

"I thought so," said Don Beltrán. "I have, therefore, spoken with Juan Velásquez de Cuéllar. He is a man of excellent reputation. He is the Royal Treasurer of King Ferdinand. He would continue your education. You would learn to be a page at court. You would meet very important people—perhaps even the King. Of course you would have to leave here for Arévalo. Think about it. There is no hurry."

How did his father know what he had been thinking about over the years? Iñigo was so happy and excited. He had dreamed for years of becoming a knight. He wanted to live with royalty. He wanted to make a name for himself. He wanted to be famous. He wanted to become rich. He wanted to honor the House of Loyola as did his brothers traveling to the Americas and dying

26

a hero's death. Everything seemed to look up for him. He couldn't have been happier. And he was very proud of himself—with his long red hair and good looks. And women began noticing him.

Soon Martín was on the road with him to Arévalo, to enlist him in the Court service of Juan Velásquez de Cuéllar. Iñigos' dreams were coming true.

11. *Don Beltrán's Death*

Then, when Iñigo was sixteen, his father died. He returned home for his father's burial. After the funeral, Magdalena, just like a mother, spoke to him. She took him to her private chapel, the little chapel where she had hung the painting of God's mother, Mary—her wedding gift from Queen Isabella.

"Iñigo," she said, "let's sit down and talk." Then they both sat in the quiet, empty chapel.

"Life, I know, is very hard at times. Your mother died after you were born. Your brothers, Juan and Beltrán, Jr., are both dead. And now, your dear father has died.

"Some people have a long life, some have a short life. Such is God's will.

"The only reason we are here on this earth is to do God's will—and then go back to Him. I believe your father and mother, and your two brothers are with God—and now, they are all watching over us, over you.

"Now, Iñigo," she continued, "there is something else I want you to know. Look at the painting of God's mother. Pray to her. She will always be there for you. The mother you never knew. She will always guard and protect you. She will make you feel happy again. All you have to do is pray to her. She will always love you and care for you as she did for her Son, Jesus."

Then Magdalena quietly got up and left Iñigo alone in front of the painting of God's mother.

And just as a dark storm with its howling wind passes over and the sun breaks through the clouds again, Iñigo got over his father's death and was on his way back to Arévalo—to become a page, a knight, a soldier for the King of Spain—to honor the House of Loyola.

12. News of Iñigo

For the next ten years, Magdalena and Martín rarely saw Iñigo. As you know, he was in the service of Juan Velásquez de Cuéllar. The years passed quickly, but, from time to time, they heard good reports of him: how he was becoming quite a gentleman, that he was kind and courteous, and that he conducted himself well in court. They heard that he was cutting quite a figure with his long red hair, and that he always dressed in the latest fashion—that he was quite the ladies' man.

Martín also heard that Iñigo got in brawls, that he was fond of drinking and gambling, but he did not tell this to Magdalena.

Then, when Iñigo was twenty-five, they learned that King Ferdinand had died and that his son, Charles V, had become King of Spain.

When Iñigo was twenty-six, news came that his sponsor, Juan Velásquez, had fallen from power for opposing the new King, and that he had died shortly after. What would become of Iñigo, Martín and Magdalena wondered.

Then news came that he had enlisted in the service of the Duke of Nájera, in the Kingdom of Navarre near the French border. There was trou-

ble there with the French, as there had been over the centuries—an age-old problem: the King of France wanted to slowly conquer Spain.

Iñigo defending Pamplona.

13. An Urgent Message to Martín

Iñigo was thirty years old when he sent a messenger to the House of Loyola, to his brother, Martín. He told the messenger to beg his brother to come with armed men to help him fight for the Duke of Nájera against the French.

"If the French conquer Pamplona, they could take over all of Spain," the messenger had told Martín.

Martín loved his brother. He decided to join him.

The next day, Magdalena watched Martín leave the House of Loyola with a group of armed men to join his brother—to fight for the Crown of Spain. She prayed that he and Iñigo would return home safely. She did not know at the time that, within a few months, Martín would return home with a handful of men, carrying Iñigo home on a stretcher.

Book 2

Pamplona

Once I turned from thee and hid,
Bound on what thou hadst forbid;
Sow the wind I would; I sinned:
I repent of what I did.

Bad I am, but yet thy child.
Father, be thou reconciled,
Spare thou me, since I see
With thy might that thou art mild.

Gerard Manley Hopkins

**Martín holding the wounded Iñigo's hand
while being carried on a stretcher.**

1. Iñigo Returns

FROM THE highest window of the House of Loyola, Magdalena saw them coming. Martín was leading a small band of men carrying someone on a stretcher. He was leading them slowly up the hill to the House of Loyola. In her heart, she knew the wounded man was Iñigo.

Quickly she prepared a bed for him with clean sheets and blankets. Then she ordered a serving woman to prepare food for the men, while she laid the table in the dining hall. She put out bowls and plates, cups and spoons for the weary men. After she put out platters of bread and cheese on the table, she went to the door and waited for Martín and the men to bring Iñigo in.

Martín looked haggard as he led the men in through the open door.

After Iñigo was carefully placed in bed, she spoke to Martín. "Martín, there is food on the table for you and the men. Go, I will attend to Iñigo."

So Martín took his men to the dining hall and fed them while Magdalena and her maid removed Iñigo's bloodstained clothes, bathed him, then put a clean sleeping gown on him.

Iñigo was in too much pain to talk while

Magdalena and her maid were caring for him. When they had finished, she said, "Rest now, Iñigo. You are home. Try to sleep."

Magdalena looked at Iñigo's face and saw tears running down his cheek, and though he couldn't speak, in gratitude he touched her hand.

Then to the servant, she said, "Dolores, please go to the surgeons in town this night. Tell them they are needed here in the morning."

2. What Happened?

The men had left to return to their wives and families while Magdalena was attending to Iñigo. She found Martín sitting alone in the dining hall. "Martín, I thank God you are back safe and sound. What happened?" she asked him. Then she took his hand and said, "Please, if you can, tell me."

"When Iñigo and I reached the city with our troops," he slowly began, "the city officials would not let us in. They wanted to negotiate with the French, because they were afraid their city would be destroyed. Iñigo was for fighting. I knew it would be suicide to stay. The citizens did not want to fight and, because of this, I did not trust them. I thought that they would turn on us—we, who had gone to help them.

"I tried to get Iñigo to leave. He would not listen. I, in anger, left. He, with a handful of men, forced his way in.

"Over twelve thousand Frenchmen were there with cannons to attack the city.

"The city council then sent a group to the French commander, André de Foix, with the terms of capitulation. He listened and agreed to the terms. He led his troops into the city. Then he

sent word to the troops in the citadel to surren-
der. They did—Herrera and his men—and left the
citadel, all except Iñigo and the men he had con-
vinced to defend Pamplona.

"The French bombarded the citadel for six
hours. When a breach in the wall was made, the
French ran in. Iñigo was waiting for them, sword
in hand. Suddenly, a cannon ball hit him between
the legs—crushing the bones of one leg and tear-
ing open the other. Iñigo went down. Pamplona
surrendered."

Magdalena listened in silence. Then she
looked into her husband's eyes and said, "But you
are safe at home. I know you love your brother.
Let us pray that God spares his life."

"Yes," said Martín, then added, "The French
treated him with much kindness. They sent in
three of their surgeons to care for him. Iñigo gave
one his dagger, another his shield, and the third
his corselet—in gratitude to them.

"After two weeks, they thought he was well
enough to travel, so they let me take him home.
We have been on the road for three weeks. It has
been five weeks since he was wounded. He can
never be a soldier again. I wonder what will
become of him."

"Rest now, Martín," Magdalena said. "You
have eaten; you have carried your brother a long
way home. Tomorrow, a surgeon will come to
attend him. Come, I will help you in bed."

3. Iñigo Grows Worse

The long journey home had not helped his broken leg. The next morning, Iñigo's condition grew worse. The surgeons came, examined his broken leg, and decided that it should be operated on again and the bones reset. At that time, there was no anesthesia, but Iñigo endured the pain without crying out or saying one word—he only clenched his fists.

After the painful surgery, one of the surgeons took Martín and Magdalena aside and said, "We have done what we could. I don't think he has much longer to live. I'm so sorry."

Martín immediately left to get a priest to give him the sacrament of the sick, but Magdalena went to her private chapel and prayed, "Dear mother Mary, Iñigo is a good man. Do not let him die. Spare his life. He is like a son to me." And then she put her hands to her face and cried for sorrow and for joy—for joy, because her husband was home again; for sorrow, because her adopted son was on his deathbed.

4. A Calm Before the Storm

The next morning, Iñigo's condition improved. The physician came again to change his dressings and could not believe it. And with each new day, his strength returned. As the weeks passed by, he tried to walk. He was able to get around—but with a limp.

You know by now that Iñigo was a very proud man. Because he limped and because the bone stuck out below his right knee—and was very noticeable—he told the surgeons to cut away some of this bone, because it embarrassed him.

Thy surgeons laughed and told him he was crazy. "If the pain of more surgery won't kill you, an infection will," one had said.

But Iñigo had his way again. The surgeons protested, but agreed to operate again.

After this third surgery, his recovery was long and painful, but what was hardest of all—he had to stay alone in bed.

5. The Big Storm

During the long months of recovery, Iñigo had to stay in bed. And most of the time he was alone. All he had was time on his hands; time to think, time to remember, time to look at his life. He did not like what he saw.

He remembered all the bad things he had done—the drinking, the brawling, the gambling.

He had wanted the life at court, the life of a soldier. He had wanted fame, honor, glory, the praise of men. He had had it all, yet he felt so empty, so dissatisfied with himself.

And the glory of battle—men killing men—how could he have enjoyed this?

He felt guilt and shame. He began to feel so badly that he wanted to kill himself. Dark thoughts and memories troubled his mind in a confusing jumble that terrified him—and they wouldn't stop.

He had been so vain, so proud, but what did this all matter now? His red hair, his stylish clothes, his fine reputation, none of this seemed to matter now.

Everything seemed so confusing. What he had thought was so important—the truth—now was a lie.

"Lord, have mercy on me, a sinner."

Killing, violence, destruction—for what? He felt disgusted with himself, he felt so ashamed of himself.

Alone in his room, he sang, "Beotibar, Beotibar, O Martín, how can we glory in war? It is wrong to kill, is it not? To take the life of a man, a brother? What of his wife and children? Yes. Let us laugh at them and kill and kill and kill." And he laughed in his agony, but his empty laughter was a cry of despair, the cry of a hopeless man. "O, God, what have I done? What have I done?"

For days, these thoughts would torment him without end. Then one day, he cried out in agony, "Lord, have mercy on me, a sinner."

6. The Confession

Magdalena had heard him and gone to his room. She saw the tears streaming down his cheeks. "Iñigo, God loves you. Why are you crying?" she asked him.

In his misery, he turned to her and said, "Oh, Magdalena, it's nothing. It's just that I feel so badly. I feel lost. I hate myself. I cannot forgive myself for what I have done, for how I have lived. My soul is in pain, not my body—and I don't know what to do. My legs are healing, but my soul is sick. I don't want to go on living."

Then Magdalena quietly left Iñigo's room. When she returned, she was carrying a picture of Mary, the painting Queen Isabella had given to her. She put the picture on Iñigo's bed and said, "Iñigo, pray to God's mother. She loves you as her own Son. She always listens to our prayers. She will heal your soul."

Iñigo took the picture and kissed it. After Magdalena left, in agony, he cried himself to sleep.

And late that night, alone in his room, he woke to see mother Mary holding the Christ Child—and she was smiling at him. He tried to talk, but could not. Mary put her finger to her lips

while she was smiling. She did not want him to wake her sleeping Child. Then in the silence, she whispered, "Be still, be silent, I understand you. This is our secret."

He felt his heart leap for joy. He felt he was washed clean, that he was whole and healthy again, that somehow she and her Child had always been with him—at home in his heart— and would always be with him. And he fell into a deep sleep, at home with himself again—and them.

7. *Nothing Counts But God*

The next morning, Magdalena carried in his breakfast. Iñigo was beaming. "Nothing counts but God," he said.

"What?" asked Magdalena, surprised at the change in his condition.

"It all makes sense," he said. "Didn't you tell me that God made us to know, love, and serve Him? Yes? Well, then it is all clear. I know what I have to do. Only God counts. It is all so very simple. Magdalena, I feel young again."

Magdalena could not believe the change that had come over Iñigo. In her happiness, she ran to get Martín. "Go to see your brother," she said. "I think he will live."

When Martín got to his room, there was Iñigo standing beside his bed. "What are you doing out of bed?" he asked, then ran to steady Iñigo as he tried to take a step.

"Learning to walk again," Iñigo said.

"But it is too soon for that!"

"I don't think so," Iñigo said. "We men of Loyola are made of iron. It is in the hills. It is in the water we drink. Let go of me, Martín. I am much stronger than you think."

"Is that so?" said Martín, secretly happy to see his brother up again.

"I can choose, I can choose, I can choose to walk or stay in bed. I can choose to serve God or men," Iñigo said. "I think I will choose to fly."

"What did Magdalena give you to drink?" Martín said. "I think you should go back to bed."

Martín helped him back to bed.

"I am so happy, Martín."

"I know, but one step at a time," Martín said before he left.

Martín later told Magdalena, "I think my brother has grown a new leg, but lost his head," but she knew that he was proud of his brother.

8. Reading and Writing

After Iñigo got through his first painful weeks of recovery (when he could do nothing but eat and sleep), Magdalena brought him two books to read—one was about the life of Christ and the other was about the lives of the Saints.

He spent many happy hours reading these books and thinking about them. He liked the book about the life of Christ so much that he copied down his favorite sentences into his notebook. The words of Jesus he copied in red ink; the words of Mary in blue ink. Each word was carefully written down. He was very proud of his penmanship. He would read from his notebook and write in it almost every day. This helped pass the time away.

And the stories of the Saints entertained him for hours. Some made him laugh, others made him cry.

He especially liked to read about St. Francis, God's Holy Fool. Francis, he thought, was a lot like himself in many ways. Francis was vain, he liked fine clothes, he was a knight, he came from a well-to-do family, but then—he left all this behind to become a beggar for Christ. Yet he was so happy and free. He found God everywhere, in all things: birds, rabbits, fish, even a wolf. And Francis talked to them all. Iñigo, too, felt that animals could understand humans, but each in its own way.

Iñigo spent many happy hours reading and dreaming about what it would be like to leave everything behind to follow Christ.

9. *Good Angels, Bad Angels*

But Iñigo had bad days, too. The pain of learning to walk again, boredom, watching other people go about their days while he was helpless and had to stay in bed—these things would depress him.

When Magdalena found him in one of his bad moods, she would talk to him.

"Iñigo," she once said, "there are good angels and bad angels. The good angels want us to feel happy, peaceful, close to God, to love ourselves. The bad angels want us to feel miserable, confused. They want us to hate ourselves and everyone else. They don't want us to know that God is always at home in our hearts even when we don't feel He is there.

"The good angels remind us that God is always there living in our hearts. Pray to them when you feel down. They will help you feel happy again—even when you have pain."

10. *Learning to Pray*

Indeed, Magdalena, like a good mother, was teaching her adopted son to pray. She was helping him to heal his soul.

And Iñigo, during the long months of recovery, was learning to talk to God. He was beginning to see everything with new eyes—the shape of an orange leaf, a glowing chestnut, a blade of grass. It was as if God was hiding in everything and everyone—Magdalena, Martín, his mule— even in a tiny thing like an ant.

And he was able to get around more—slowly, of course.

One day, Martín saw him putting a chair next to his mule.

"Stop!" hollered Martín. "You will fall and break both legs."

But Iñigo stood on the chair and whispered into the mule's ear, "Let's show him how we can work together. Let's show him we can do it. Let's show him you've got more brains than he has."

And the mule stood still while Iñigo slowly mounted him from the chair. And then, the mule carefully gave Iñigo a ride without knocking over the chair!

11. Brother to Brother

After Iñigo got back from his ride, Martín found him feeding the mule in the stable.

"Where did you go?" asked Martín.

"I went to visit the Garíns. They did so much for me when I lived with them. I wanted to thank them and to say goodbye."

"Oh?" asked Martín. "Are you planning to leave the House of Loyola?"

"Yes," answered Iñigo. "In a few weeks, Pero and I want to travel to Navarrete. I want to see the Duke of Nájera again. Maybe I can be of service to him."

"You can hardly walk," said Martín. "I don't want you to go. You are not strong enough to travel. I don't want to see those surgeons operating on your leg again."

"It is healing, Martín. I know I can't run, but that doesn't mean I should stay in bed."

"I disagree," said Martín. "The House of Loyola is where you belong. You know you are welcome here." Then he added, "Even Magdalena thinks you are pushing too hard."

"You worry too much, Martín. I am getting along just fine. God is with me all the way."

"Was God with you when that cannonball hit your legs?" asked Martín.

"Yes," answered Iñigo.

12. The Secret

The weeks passed by quickly. It had taken Iñigo over a half a year to recover, and he was anxious to be on the road again with Pero, his brother.

Pero was now a priest. He was the one who told Martín not to be so obstinate, but to let Iñigo go to Navarrete. "I will be with him," he had said. "I will take good care of him."

"Well then, go," Martín had said. "I can't stop you or him."

But before Iñigo and Pero left for Navarrete, Iñigo wanted to speak with Magdalena. He found her in her private chapel praying. She was alone.

He went inside and knelt down next to her. "Magdalena," he said, " I have something very important to tell you.

"Magdalena," he continued, "I feel in my heart that God wants me to go to Jerusalem. I want to visit Bethlehem where Jesus was born, Nazareth where He grew up, and the mountain where He ascended into Heaven—they say His footprints are still there!

"But most of all, I want to be a beggar. I want to depend only on God. I want to live in the Holy

Land and serve the people. I have been thinking about this for months, but I haven't told anyone.

"I am going to Barcelona to catch a ship for the Holy Land. On my way, I want to spend a night at Montserrat. I want to pray there before the Madonna and Child—to help me live my new life.

"At Montserrat, I am going to leave my sword and dagger on the altar. There I will make my promise to God and His mother that I will only follow their will in all I do.

"Then I plan to buy a poor pilgrim's robe and sandals, to wear them, and give away my fine clothes to the poor. Afterward, I will make my way to Barcelona bound for Jerusalem. This is my plan. I want to live in poverty as Francis lived.

"Please, don't tell Martín what I have told you. He wouldn't understand. He already thinks I'm crazy. He would ride to stop me. You know how much he is against my going to Navarrete with Pero.

"Tomorrow morning, Pero and I are leaving together. We plan to stop at Oñate to visit our sister. I will leave Pero there and go on to see the Duke alone. Then I will make my way to the Holy Land. God will be my only guide—and the good angels. Pero is in on all this, too.

"Magdalena, thank you for everything you have done for me. Please, don't cry. I know I will see you again, though I don't know when. God will be with me all the way."

Magdalena did not know what to say, but she knew she must not get in God's way. She simply said, "I understand. *Vaya con Dios, mi hijo,*" which means *Go with God, my son.*

And so Iñigo left Magdalena alone in the chapel. He knew that she would always be praying for him—and Martín.

Book 3

A New Life

I have life before me still
And thy purpose to fulfil;
Yea a debt to pay thee yet:
Help me, sir, and so I will.

But thou bidst, and just thou art,
Me shew mercy from my heart
Towards my brother, ever other
Man my mate and counterpart.

Gerard Manley Hopkins

Iñigo promised to serve only Christ and
His mother.

1. Montserrat

WHEN IÑIGO left the House of Loyola this time, he left as a new man. His desires for the life of the court, the life of a soldier—all hopes for fame, glory, honor—were dead. A cannonball to the leg had helped with that.

He was thirty-one when he left the House of Loyola and set out for the Holy Land. True to the secret he shared with Magdalena, he was on the back of a mule on his way to the mountains of Montserrat.

High in the rocky crags of these mountains, the church still stands. In this church is a very old statue of Mary holding the Christ Child. It is black from the smoke of hundreds of thousands of candles people have lit while praying there. This statue is called the Black Madonna. It is here that Iñigo was on his way to pray.

Before he got there, he stopped in a town along the way. There he bought a pilgrim's robe of very rough cloth, a gourd to carry water, and a staff to help him walk on his journey. These were the only things he planned to take with him on his way to the Holy Land.

When Iñigo finally got to Montserrat, he went into the church. He found a priest and made his Confession to him. After his Confession, he met the priest outside of church and gave his sword and dagger to him—and also his mule.

Then, without anyone seeing him, he took off his rich clothing and put on the rough pilgrim's gown. And when he saw a beggar, he gave his fine clothes to him.

Then Iñigo went back into the church. In front of the Black Madonna of Montserrat, Iñigo promised to serve only Christ and His mother.

2. Manresa

Now he was ready to continue his journey to the Holy Land. His first stop was Manresa. He lived there for about a year. When he was not begging for food or taking care of sick people in the hospital, he spent much time alone talking to God. He let his hair grow long and wild. He no longer cared what people thought about him.

One of his favorite spots in Manresa was near the River Cardoner. He used to sit in the caves along the river bank and watch the river flow by and think about God. He felt God in the river. He heard God in the birds singing. And when he looked at sweet smelling flowers, they reminded him of God.

He used to tell others, "You can find God in all things—in everything you taste, touch, hear, smell, and see. You can find God in all things—even in a blade of grass, an orange leaf."

And, watching the stars at night, he understood in his heart that God made all things, that He made all things good, and that He hated nothing that He had made.

Once he saw God as a great white light, with rays coming out of this light, and that you and I—that everything God made—are made out of this light. It was hard for him to explain, but he said, "God is in everything." He felt all of this so strongly inside that he said, "I would rather die than lie about all that I feel and understand."

3. *Barcelona and Rome*

Iñigo's next stop was Barcelona. He got very sick there and almost died. It was a very cold winter that year, but many good people took care of him. They even gave him two dark grey jackets, a warm cap, and good shoes for the journey. The shipmaster even gave him free passage to Rome, but made him promise to take along enough food for himself for the journey.

Soon he was on a boat to Rome. Once there, he got permission from the Pope to go to the Holy Land. Then he was on another boat to Jerusalem and spent many days at sea. Again, he got very sick, but he felt in his heart that God was leading him all the way. And so He was; soon Iñigo was stepping off the boat onto the shores of the Holy Land.

4. The Holy Land

Iñigo visited the places where Christ was born, where Christ taught the people, where He died, where He rose from the dead, and where He ascended to heaven. His dream, to live there and speak to others about God—to be of help to souls—was coming true. But he soon found out that this dream was not part of God's plan. After a month in Jerusalem, the chief official told him he could not stay, because it was too dangerous for him to live there. Iñigo disagreed, but was ordered to leave.

So Iñigo the beggar, the pilgrim, the friend of God, had to leave Jerusalem and return to Spain. It was on his long journey back to Spain that he kept wondering how he could best serve Christ and His mother. The idea came to him that he could be of better help to souls if he had an education. So he decided that he would go to school in Barcelona.

5. Years of Study

In Barcelona, he went to school and studied Latin and grammar. Most of the students were less than half his age. Yes, he was embarrassed. At his age, it was not easy to begin studying again, but he tried hard and passed his exams. He did well. His teachers encouraged him to go to the University of Alcalá to study philosophy and the arts. So Iñigo enrolled in the University of Alcalá.

While he was studying at the University of Alcalá, as you might guess, he talked about God with almost everyone who would listen. When the officials found out he was doing this, they put him in jail. They proclaimed he had no right to talk about God. What did he know? He had not even graduated. He did not study theology. And why would God talk to him? He was a beggar, no saint! He owned nothing!

They kept him in prison for forty-two days, but when they were done questioning him, they could find nothing lawfully wrong with what he said or did. However, upon his release, they forbade him to talk about God until he had studied philosophy and theology, and they told him to dress as a student, that is, in a black gown. So

Iñigo put on a black gown, combed his hair, and decided to move from Alcalá and to study in Salamanca. Certainly he could talk to people about God there!

Iñigo moved to Salamanca and continued to study there. But again, in Salamanca, too, the authorities got angry with him because he talked about God. Again they put him in jail.

They questioned him for long hours, but could find nothing wrong with what he did or said. Many people visited him in jail, because they felt closer to God after talking with him. Then, after twenty-two days in jail, the officials released him. They told him he could talk about God, but that he must never mention evil or sin.

Iñigo concluded he was not welcome in Salamanca. He remembered hearing that people were more open-minded in Paris. He would not have to be afraid of talking about God there. So he decided to go to France—on foot—to study in Paris.

6. Paris

Iñigo the pilgrim, the searcher, the beggar, the prisoner, the friend of Jesus, found his way to Paris. He began his studies at the University of Paris. He also made many friends who wanted to join him in his work of telling others about God. They often met together. Their names were Pierre Favre, Francis Xavier, Diego Laínez, Simáo Rodríguez, Alonso Salmerón, and Nicolás Bobadilla.

Then at the age of forty-four, Iñigo got his degree. He became "Master Ignatius of Loyola, of the diocese of Pamplona."

Iñigo's health was never good. The many years of travel and studying had taken its toll on him. His friends knew he needed a rest. They suggested he return home to the House of Loyola. And so he set out. He walked from Paris to Azpeitia (the little town near the House of Loyola), a distance of five hundred and fifty miles. He hadn't seen his family for thirteen years.

7. The House of Loyola

"He is back," Martín told Magdalena, after seeing Iñigo in Azpeitia.

Martín was in a bad mood. As you remember, Iñigo had left thirteen years earlier without telling Martín where he was truly going. An old friend had told Martín that he saw Iñigo at the hospital outside of Azpeitia. When Martín went to see Iñigo at the hospital, Iñigo had refused to come to stay at the House of Loyola.

"Who, Martín?" Magdalena asked.

"Master Ignatius de Loyola of the diocese of Pamplona."

"He is? Where is he?" asked Magdalena. "When did you see him?"

"Just now. He is staying at the hospital next to the river. He came from Paris with a Master's degree. He looks like a beggar in his pilgrim's gown and sandals. He is a disgrace to the House of Loyola. I found him talking to sick people in the hospital. I could not convince him to come home. He told me that it was God's will that he stay there."

"You should be proud of him, Martín. He is doing God's work. People are hungry for God. He is feeding them."

"Now you sound like a nun," answered Martín.

"Martín, God loves all his children—the sick, the poor, the needy. Iñigo is bringing God's love to them. He is caring for those nobody else cares for. I must see him."

"Go then, see your adopted son."

"Please, come with me."

"No, the sight of him dressed as a beggar sickens me."

"Then you will not come?"

"No," answered Martín.

8. Magdalena's Visit

The courtyard of the hospital was crowded with people. Some had even climbed into the branches of the plum trees to see and hear Iñigo talking about God. Magdalena was there, too, listening to him. After Iñigo had finished, the crowd quietly dispersed. Some people left for home, others went to the chapel to pray.

When Iñigo noticed Magdalena, his eyes filled with tears. Slowly he limped over to her.

"Mother, Magdalena, it is so good to see you," he said. "Please, sit down. We must visit."

"Yes," said Magdalena, as she sat on one of the benches under a plum tree.

Iñigo sat on a bench opposite her.

"Many years have passed, my son," she said.

"Yes," he answered.

"I can see that you are very happy," she said. "Your dreams are coming true—to serve God and His mother. I have not forgotten what you told me many years ago."

"Yes, Magdalena, and you must also know that I have met six others who wish to do what I do. They were the ones who told me to go home for a rest. We call ourselves *los compañeros de Jesús*—the friends of Jesus. As soon as I am well enough, I will join them in Venice. We all want to serve God by helping others find Him. It is all very simple."

"Will you and your friends be like the Franciscans, the Dominicans—with rules and laws?"

"I haven't really thought about that yet," answered Iñigo. "To me, the only law one should follow is the law of love the Holy Spirit writes in the heart."

"In that sense, Iñigo, I am a *Compañera de Jesús.*"

Iñigo thought for a moment and then said, "Yes, you are. Everyone is, but many must be reminded of it." He was smiling.

Then he turned serious and said, "Magdalena, I know I have disappointed Martín, but I have God's work to do."

"I understand," answered Magdalena. "I remember when I first met you. You were only seven years old. The first time I laid eyes on you I felt God had something very special in mind for you. Now I know that is true.

"And I know what I must do, too. I promise you, I will be a good wife to Martín, your brother, and a good mother to our children. That is what God wants me to do." She was smiling.

"My prayers are with you always, Magdalena. I am forever grateful to you for raising me and nursing me back to health."

"And my prayers are always with you—in everything you do—for the greater honor and glory of God."

Magdalena rose to leave. Iñigo walked with her to the door of the courtyard. As she left, she turned and said, "Iñigo, don't worry about Martín. He secretly admires what you are doing, though he cannot understand you."

After Iñigo got his health back, he sent word to Martín that he was leaving for Venice. When Martín heard this, he insisted on accompanying Iñigo to the province border—and that Iñigo ride a horse. Iñigo accepted this, but at the border, he embraced his brother, got off the horse, and began his journey to Venice on foot—penniless.

9. The Final Years

Iñigo became a priest at the age of forty-six in Venice. His six friends were with him. Now he could teach others about God without being put in jail for doing this.

But then, the authorities again got angry with him and his friends for banding together and teaching others about God. They said he needed official approval.

So Iñigo had to visit the Pope. Pope Paul III allowed Iñigo, then forty-nine, and his friends to officially work together as *La Compañía de Jesús*. Oh, but he was happy that day! He knew in his heart that this is what God wanted him to do—and he was doing it. And there were more surprises for him.

From all over the world, men, both young and old, came to Rome to join his *Compañía de Jesús*. Like Iñigo, each wanted to serve God and His mother. He treated them all as his sons—or even grandsons. They all were amazed at the kindness and respect he showed each of them.

He was kept very busy with all these new *compañeros*. Each morning, he would say, "What shall we do for God today?"

Once, when he learned that a young man

**He even did a Basque dance to cheer
the young man up.**

from the Basque country (where he himself was born) was sick, he made a Basque meal and carried it to him. He even did a Basque dance to cheer the young man up.

Eventually, with so many men joining his *Compañía de Jesús,* he had to write down rules, but he reiterated that the most important rule that each should follow was the law of love that the Holy Spirit writes in each one's heart.

As an old man, Iñigo was sure of two things: everything changes, but God's love is always here. Some days he was so very happy; other days he was very sad. Some days people were kind to him; other days they treated him cruelly. But, somehow, God was always there. Yes, he had found out that moods change like the weather, like the clothes we wear, but God's love is always there. Often he would say, "What new kind of life is this that we are now beginning?"

Along with another great friend of God, Teresa of Avila, he could truly say,

> *Let nothing frighten you.*
> *Let nothing shake you.*
> *Everything passes.*
> *God does not change.*
> *Who trusts in God, lacks nothing.*
> *God is enough.*

Iñigo died—or went "back home,"—at the age

of sixty-five. But his spirit lives on in all those who have a reverence for life and a respect for all that God has made—those who have found God in all things.

Today, the *Compañía de Jesús* is called the Society of Jesus, and the men, the Jesuits.

THE END